To Brecken –
Love,
Auntie.
Angie

To all the children at
Lancaster Free Methodist Church   S.J.D.

Text copyright © 2010 Sarah J. Dodd
Illustrations copyright © 2010 Dubravka Kolanovic
This edition copyright © 2010 Lion Hudson

The moral rights of the author and illustrator
have been asserted

A Lion Children's Book
an imprint of
**Lion Hudson plc**
Wilkinson House, Jordan Hill Road,
Oxford OX2 8DR, England
www.lionhudson.com
ISBN 978 0 7459 6209 2

First edition 2010
1 3 5 7 9 10 8 6 4 2 0

A catalogue record for this book is available
from the British Library

Typeset in 18/23 Goudy Old Style BT
Printed in China April 2010 (manufacturer LH06)

Distributed by:
UK: Marston Book Services Ltd, PO Box 269, Abingdon, Oxon OX14 4YN
USA: Trafalgar Square Publishing, 814 N Franklin Street, Chicago, IL 60610
USA Christian Market: Kregel Publications, PO Box 2607, Grand Rapids, MI 49501

# Bible Stories for
# Little Angels

Sarah J. Dodd

Dubravka Kolanovic

LION
CHILDREN'S

# When the world began

In the beginning, God made the world. Sunshine warmed it, plants covered it, and animals and birds filled it with play and song. God made people to enjoy this wonderful world – a man called Adam, and a woman called Eve.

God planted a beautiful garden and gave them everything they needed, because he loved them. "You may eat the fruit from any tree in the garden, except one," God said.

Eve looked at the tree God showed them. The fruit looked tasty.

"It's not safe to eat," warned God. "If you eat it, you will have to leave my garden."

One day, the snake slithered up to Eve. "God isn't telling the truth," he hissed. "That fruit is the best you will ever eat. Go on – try some."

Eve picked the fruit and ate it. She gave some to Adam. "It's delicious," she said. So Adam ate it too.

Almost at once, they knew they had done wrong. They tried to hide from God, but he found them. "Now you will have to leave the garden," said God. He was very sad.

God sent Adam and Eve outside the garden. Angels guarded the gate. The light around them was so bright that nobody could come near it to get back in.

"We'll have to try to grow our own fruit and vegetables out here," sighed Adam as he looked at the weeds and the hard, dry soil. "This is going to be hard work!"

But God still loved the people he had made. He began to make a plan to fix the wrong thing they had done and let all people be his friends again.

# Noah listens to God

Adam and Eve had children. These children had their own families, and so the number of people grew. But they all liked to argue and fight. Only one man was good. His name was Noah, and he loved God.

"Listen to me," God said to Noah. "I will make it rain like it's never rained before. You must build an enormous boat, called an ark."

"Are you sure?" asked Noah, looking at the cloudless sky.

"Listen to me," said God, and he told Noah how to build the ark and what to take on board.

"How silly!" laughed Noah's neighbours as he began to build. "Your boat will never float. There's no water!"

*Drip.*

The rain began to fall.

*Drip. Drop.*

Noah herded every kind of animal into the ark, just as God had said.

Noah and his family went into the ark, and God shut the door.

The rain poured down. Mountains disappeared beneath the water, and the ark floated over them.

At last, the rain stopped. The ark bumped onto the top of a mountain and got stuck there. "I wonder if there is dry land anywhere?" said Noah.

He sent a dove to fly over the flood. The dove returned with a leafy twig in its beak, so Noah knew that somewhere a tree must be growing.

The water began to go down.

Noah heaved open the door of the ark. The animals hopped, jumped, and wriggled out. Noah and his family stepped into a clean, fresh world.

God painted a rainbow in the sky. "Listen to me," he said. "I promise I will never make another flood like that."

# Abraham and the promise

Abraham and his wife, Sarah, had a good life. They lived in a land where there was plenty of grass for all their sheep and goats. But they were sad. They longed for a child to love and look after.

"I will give you a baby boy," God promised Abraham. "He will be the beginning of my special family. There will be more people in this family than there are stars in the sky."

"I believe you," said Abraham.

Abraham waited a long, long time. Nothing happened. "God always keeps his promises," thought Abraham, so he waited some more.

Sarah was not so sure. "I am getting old," she sighed. "I don't think I will ever be a mother."

One day, Abraham was sitting at the door of his tent when three visitors appeared.

"Sarah!" called Abraham. "We must welcome them! Will you bake some bread and prepare a meal?"

Sarah brought food to the visitors and left them talking to Abraham. But she stayed nearby so she could listen to what they were saying.

"Next year we will come back," said one of the visitors, "and by then you will have your own little boy."

Sarah burst out laughing. She was too old for babies! Those strangers were talking nonsense!

"Why are you laughing?" asked the visitor. "Nothing is too hard for God."

Abraham and Sarah realized the visitors were angels. The following year, Sarah had a baby boy, just as the angels had said.

Abraham called the baby Isaac. He smiled as he held his new son. "God always keeps his promises," he said.

# The baby in a basket

God's special family grew, just as he promised. Isaac's grandchildren and their families moved to Egypt, where there was plenty of food for everybody.

But as the years went by, they were no longer welcome. The new king of Egypt made them work hard on his building sites.

"There are just too *many* of these people!" declared the king. "We must do something about it!" He ordered that all their baby boys must be thrown into the river.

One mother was determined to keep her baby safe. She took a basket and made it waterproof. Then she put her baby inside and floated the basket in the reeds at the edge of the river.

"You stay here," she said to her daughter, Miriam. "Watch over your baby brother."

"What if a crocodile comes?" gulped Miriam.

"God will keep the baby safe," said her mother.

The king's daughter liked to bathe in that place. She came down to the river with her servants.

"I can see something," said the princess, pointing at the basket. The baby began to cry. "Poor little thing! He is all alone. I will call him Moses." The princess picked up baby Moses, then shook her head. "But I don't know how to look after a baby!"

Miriam jumped out of her hiding place. "I know someone who can help!" she said, and she ran to fetch her mother.

"Will you look after this baby for me?" asked the princess.

Moses' mother hugged him tightly. "Of course I will," she said, and she quietly thanked God for keeping them all safe.

# Daniel in danger

The family of Abraham and Moses grew bigger than ever. They knew it was right to love God and do as he asked them. They trusted God, even when they were taken to a faraway land.

A young man named Daniel worked for the king. The king liked him, but the other servants were jealous.

"We must find a way to get rid of Daniel," they muttered.

So the servants went to the king. "You are the greatest!" they said. "You should make a rule that nobody is allowed to worship anyone except you."

The king liked this idea. He felt important. "But what if somebody worships God?" he asked.

"Throw him to the lions!" cackled the servants.

Daniel did not want to break any rules, but he knew that God was more important than the king. Three times every day he prayed at an open window, where everyone could see.

The servants hurried to tell the king. "Remember the rule!" they hissed. "Daniel must be thrown to the lions."

The king was upset, but he knew that he must keep his word, or nobody would ever listen to him.

The king kept his lions in a great pit. His servants threw Daniel in. The lions were hungry; they were sure to eat Daniel.

The king was so worried that he couldn't sleep all night. When morning came, he rushed to the lion pit.

To his astonishment, Daniel was safe! "God sent an angel to protect me," explained Daniel. "The lions didn't even open their mouths."

The king was delighted. "Your God is amazing!" he said.

# A baby like no other

It was a busy night in Bethlehem. The inns were crowded with travellers, and the sound of laughter and feasting spilled onto the streets.

It was a quiet night in the fields. Sheep called to their lambs and the shepherds dozed by the fire, wishing something exciting would happen.

Suddenly a dazzling angel appeared in the sky. The shepherds were terrified. Perhaps a quiet night was better after all!

"Don't be afraid," said the angel. "I've come to tell you that a special baby has been born. He's the one God has been planning to send from the beginning. He will show people how to be friends with God again."

Thousands more angels crammed the sky, all singing for joy.

"Go to Bethlehem," said the first angel. "You'll know which baby it is. He will be lying in a manger."

The angels disappeared.

"In a *manger*?" said the shepherds. "Animals eat out of mangers. You don't put babies in them!"

Shaking their heads, they left the sheep and hurried to Bethlehem. They peered down all the alleys and back streets. At last, just as the angel had said, they found a newborn baby sleeping in a manger in the middle of a stable.

"His name is Jesus," whispered the baby's mother. "He is a baby like no other. He is God's Son."

The baby slept as visitors crept in to see him. Angels crowded round the roof, their song as gentle as the night-time breeze.

The shepherds knelt in the straw and realized that sometimes the greatest things in the world happen on a quiet night.

# Wild weather

When Jesus grew up, he travelled around telling people about God. One day, he was walking by a lake when he saw four fishermen – Simon and his brother Andrew were catching fish from the lake with a net; James and his brother John were in their boat getting ready to fish.

"Come with me," said Jesus. "I will teach you to catch people instead of fish."

"What does he mean?" whispered Andrew. "Does he want us to catch people and put them in prison?"

Simon roared with laughter. "No! He wants us to help bring people into God's family."

Andrew frowned. "What do you think? Should we go?"

Simon looked at his beloved boat. He looked at Jesus. "Yes," he said. "I'm ready for an adventure."

The four fishermen became good friends with Jesus. They saw him do amazing things – he made sick people well; he made sad people happy; he made lonely people feel loved.

One night, Jesus and his friends were sailing across the lake. Jesus was asleep in the back of the boat when a storm blew up.

The wind howled and the waves leaped. Water began to fill the boat, but Jesus slept on.

"Wake up!" yelled his friends. "We're going to sink!"

Jesus stood up in the boat like an extra mast. "Be quiet!" he said to the wind. "Be still," he said to the waves. At once the lake was calm.

"You don't have to be scared of anything," said Jesus. "God will always take care of you."

# Jesus helps a little girl

Rebekah did not feel well. Her head hurt and she was too hot. "Lie down on your bed," said Rebekah's mother. "You'll feel better soon."

But Rebekah didn't feel better; she felt worse. Her friends came, laughing and chattering, to see if she wanted to play.

"Be quiet!" said Rebekah's mother. "Rebekah is very ill."

The children sat outside the door, their faces worried and their voices low.

"I know someone who can help," said Rebekah's father. "I will go and fetch Jesus." And away he ran.

Rebekah's eyes grew heavy. Her mother held her hand. The day was hot and the room was still as poor Rebekah grew weaker and weaker… and died.

"It is too late!" sobbed Rebekah's mother. "What can Jesus do now?"

The children huddled round the door began to cry. Their mothers heard the news and came, weeping and wailing, to share in the sadness.

Jesus arrived in a hurry with Rebekah's father. "Don't weep," he said to the mothers. "Don't cry," he said to the children. "Your friend is only sleeping."

Jesus went into the house. He took Rebekah's lifeless hand and said, "Little girl, get up!"

Rebekah's parents gasped as she opened her eyes and sat up. She was alive!

"What's happening?" called the children. "Can we come in?"

As soon as they were allowed in, the children rushed to the bed and hugged their friend.

"Nothing is too difficult for Jesus!" said Rebekah's mother with a smile.

# Jesus and the children

Joshua stood at the back of a jostling crowd. All he could see were legs.

"I wish we could get closer," grumbled Joshua's mother. "I want Jesus to meet you."

Joshua sighed. He knew Jesus must be a very important person, but he was tired of people treading on his toes.

As the grown-ups began to leave, Joshua pushed forward with some other children.

"Oh, no you don't." Jesus' friends stood in the way. "Jesus is a very important person. He won't want to waste his time with children."

"Actually," called Jesus, "I'd love to see the children. They belong to God."

Joshua found himself face to face with a kind-looking man.

"You are a *very important person* to God," said Jesus. "Let me tell you a story."

Everyone pushed closer to listen. Joshua sat on Jesus' knee.
"There was a farmer who had a hundred sheep," began Jesus.
"One of them got lost. Most farmers would say, 'Never mind, I still
have ninety-nine sheep,' but this farmer loved *all* his sheep. He
searched everywhere for the missing one. When he found it, he
carried it home, just like this." Jesus lifted Joshua onto his shoulder.
Joshua giggled.

"The farmer was so happy, he threw a party!" said Jesus.
"When any of you choose to become God's friend, all the angels
dance for joy!" He lifted Joshua down and smiled. "*Everyone* is
important to God."

# A sad day, a glad day

Joshua was in a crowd again. But this time he was at the front, waving a huge palm branch like a flag. Jesus was coming to Jerusalem, where the most important people lived.

Everyone cheered when Jesus arrived, riding on a donkey. Some people rushed forward to lay their cloaks on the ground like a royal carpet. "Hooray!" they shouted. "Jesus is the king God promised us!"

But Joshua saw that Jesus looked sad, as though something bad was going to happen.

A few days later, Joshua was playing in front of his house when his father came home with bad news. "The important people in Jerusalem have done a terrible thing," he said. "They told lies about Jesus and said he had done bad things. Their soldiers nailed him to a wooden cross to die. It's the worst punishment of all."

Joshua cried all that day, and the next.

The following day, Joshua's family got up just as the sun began to light the sky. They hurried to the quiet garden in Jerusalem where Jesus' body had been laid. They wanted to say goodbye. But someone else had got there first...

"That's Mary, one of Jesus' best friends," whispered Joshua's mother. "But who is that man she's talking to? I can't see his face."

Joshua jumped up. "It's Jesus!" he cried.

"It can't be!" gasped his mother.

But it truly was. And Jesus had a special message for everyone:
"I am going back to heaven soon. I will be alive forever, and
one day I will come back and take you there to live with me.
Now anyone can be friends with God!"